FROM A TEACHER TO STUDENTS

I GOT THIS

WORKBOOK

AFFIRMATIONS FOR TEENS TO RELIEVE STRESS
AND CREATE AN AWESOME SCHOOL YEAR

ANDRENE BONNER

SISAL
PUBLISHING

New York

I Got This:

AFFIRMATIONS FOR TEENS TO RELIEVE STRESS AND CREATE AN AWESOME SCHOOL YEAR

contact@sisalpublishing.com.

www.sisalpublishing.com

Published by: Sisal Publishing

Library of Congress Cataloging in Publication Data

Book Developer: Faith Nelson, Watercourse LLC

Cover Design by Les Solot

Interior Design by Oseyi Okoeguale

ISBN 13 978-0-9975905-5-5 (paperback)

ISBN 10: 0-9975905-5-6

Bonner, Andrene, 1955-

Author's Photograph by Yvonne Taylor [From Author's Personal Archives]

Printed in the United States of America

First Edition:

Publisher's Disclaimer

I Got This: Affirmation for Teens to Relieve Stress and Create an Awesome School Year is a work of non-fiction. The author has drawn on her personal life experiences as a teacher to create Affirmations for students to shape their thinking about success in school and career. This book is not intended as a substitute for the medical advice of physicians. The reader should regularly consult a physician in matters relating to his or her health and particularly with respect to any symptoms that may require diagnosis or medical attention.

Dedicated to

Kyle Graham

FROM THE EDITOR

How does a teenager say no to grandma when she asks you to edit a book written for teens? You don't say no, you just surrender to her request and get it done.

I am about to enter the 12th grade in the fall of 2019 and all I have on my mind is college. How does a book of Affirmations and journal exercises get into the mix?

Well, I wish I had this book when I was in middle school. It is the time when teens are most self-conscious about failure.

My grandma talked me through the first draft of the book and then emailed me a copy. When I started reading, I realized that the language was way too formal for our age group. Granted, by now, we are exposed to most forms of writing for different audiences. I told her that this book needs to be more relaxed. That is when my editor's pen rolled across the pages.

There is so much to like about this book. Reading an Affirmations every day gives you a sense of routine. From the *situations* to the *Journals*, we are given the opportunity to talk and work our way to success.

Then she continued, "Can you write me an app for the book?" I said, it's a good idea, I can introduce you to a few apps that we young people are listening to and you can make your judgment about which one will work for your book.

My grandma is a character. What will she think of next?

Enjoy.

Jamaya Maynard

LETTER TO PARENTS

Dear Parents:

Students are facing challenges all the time, big and small. Yes, they also create problems and challenges for themselves. However, the bigger question is, are they being derailed by these challenges.

I Got This: Affirmations for Students to Relieve Stress and Create an Awesome School Year captures some challenging scenarios students sometimes experience and their frustrations as they try to cope. The workbook has some easy to understand exercises your child can explore with your help. These exercises deliver results. For the parent whose child has had some measure of success over the years, there may be days that will stretch the limits of your child's confidence. This book can be useful.

I Got This: Affirmations for Students to Relieve Stress and Create an Awesome School Year is designed to help your child manage overwhelm by motivating him or her to complete tasks and find solutions to problems that seem impossible to overcome.

I invite you and your child to read and talk about the first section of the book, *Welcome to the Process*. It outlines what your child can expect from Day One and many ways to use the book to experience success.

Enjoy the school year, knowing that your child is able to draw on affirmations that will transform his or her way of thinking about school, college and career.

Best regards,

Andrene Bonner

The appearance of things changes according to
the emotions; and thus we see magic and beauty in them,
while the magic and beauty are really in ourselves.

Khalil Gibran (January 6, 1883 - April 10, 1931)

TABLE OF CONTENTS

WELCOME TO THE PROCESS

School is very rewarding but it can be just as stressful. It is my hope that you manage the stress, discover your awesomeness and have a successful school year.

Success is measured by the choices you make. Therefore, this year, you get to choose to be the superhero in your story. Think about your favorite superhero for a moment. This person has the discipline to prepare his or her mind and body for the challenge; has the courage to face the monster, the challenges and the unknown to fight for what he or she believes in; is so prepared that he or she knows what strategies to use during the battle; has enough strength and empathy to help others; and finally, knows when to go to his or her cave and rest. No worries. This could be you. You have the potential and you have help. You are not alone!

I Got This: *Affirmations For Teens to Relieve Stress and Create an Awesome School Year* is a guide for students to discover their inner superhero, their inborn courage and strength. Its purpose is to help students practice positive self-talk, avoid overwhelm, relieve stress, maintain focus, accomplish daily tasks, take personal responsibility, discover their own unique learning styles, become skillful in the required subjects and make sense of the world.

Each chapter in this book first lays the foundation by mirroring some key areas in the syllabus your teacher will give you on the first day of the school year. However, the book provides much more. There are three sections: **Situations, Affirmations** and **journal.**

The **Situations** are just some of the events and dilemmas that so many students have faced during the school year. The Affirmations help you best respond to these and other Situations. The **journal** section provides the space for you to write about your feelings and list your To-Dos and accomplishments.

Affirmations! What are those? Affirmations are declarations you repeat to awaken your inner genius. They serve as motivation to help you change your attitude and make the best choices. Affirmations also help you to visualize your goals more clearly and become more mindful.

Let's look more closely at ways in which you can activate Affirmations during your day. When you wake in the morning, focus on an Affirmation for 60 seconds, two or three minutes to get into a success mindset. Do it longer if you can. Look at yourself in the mirror and stare deep into your eyes and repeat the Affirmation. For example, whisper or say out loud with feeling before your exam, "I am calm. I know what to write on the exam because I studied. I got this." If you feel self-conscious about being disturbed or interrupted by family members, find a quiet spot in the home whether the bathroom or closet.

Another opportunity to use Affirmations is while walking or being driven to school. Plug in headphones or earbuds and repeat the Affirmation over your most loved beat from a playlist. Do this until it awakens your confidence hormones. You can do the same thing on your restroom break at school. This practice is perfectly suited for the quiz, examination and science lab day when confidence seems out of reach. You can do it. How do I know?

Successful young people like Yara Shahidi on the popular TV series *Blackish* and *Grownish* use Affirmation to motivate herself and stay grounded. Oprah Winfrey, Kristen Bell, Jennifer Aniston, Justin Bieber, Lebron James, Katy Perry, Steph Curry among others use this kind of positive self-talk to either start their day or get them through tough times.

Take the time to write in the journal section of the book. Write about your feelings, what you are discovering about yourself and your own learning. You can keep your journal private and read it over and over again. Use it to make adjustments in your daily life and just watch yourself create the most awesome school year.

If you spend one week on each Affirmation and write a journal entry you should cover forty principles, just the amount of weeks in the traditional school year. Some school systems have longer spans but you can use this system like a box of Legos, pulling apart, reconstructing and retrofitting this model to work for you. Here are ten key strategies below:

 Sometimes you get up in the morning and decision-making is hard. You want it to be as easy as brushing your teeth. Just open the book at any page and choose the Affirmation in that section.

 Browse the table of contents once per week or every day and choose the Affirmation that focuses on your priorities and your most urgent needs.

 You don't have to memorize the Affirmations, use your smartphone. Take a picture of it or enter it in the reminder section. Go old-school and scribble the Affirmation on a piece of paper and put it in your pocket.

We increase our stress when we are disorganized. *I Got This* can help you to plan your year no matter the assignment. Use the journal section in the book as a day planner and break down assignments into manageable portions – research, drafting and editing.

 Do you have group assignments and have trouble working with team members? Is the little gremlin on your shoulder screaming, "I can't stand X!" or asking, "What is Y talking about?" You can't change them but what can you do to improve the situation? Find Affirmations like those on pages 21 and 27 to help you communicate with team members and get the assignment done.

 You are an AP Literature student and you got the dreaded summer reading assignment that you will be tested on when you return to school in August or September. You know you don't want to do anything in the summer. Fine. Use the journal to strategize. Have your parents purchase the book in the spring and start reading early. Otherwise, borrow the books from your local library. Depending on your library's schedule, you could even borrow the book twice during the summer. In either situation, use the Affirmations to cut down overwhelm. You can declare something like this: "I am organized. I am smart. Research is easy for me."

 Summer School presents a problem for some students because it's an eighteen week semester compressed into six weeks or less. Furthermore, without this summer school course, the student can't go to the next grade level, graduate or get admitted to college. This book provides critical support at this stage because it gives you strategies to:

    a. combat overwhelm

    b. maintain focus

    c. get the work done

    d. reward yourself with an awesome summer

 You can go at your own pace because this book is designed to be used as a supplement alongside your teacher's daily classroom instructions. In other words, you don't have to follow the daily and seasonal directions. Nor do you have to do the book sequentially. For example, you may read an Affirmation and get Spidey senses about it. It feels right. You can stay on that Affirmation for weeks, even the whole semester.

- You can make your own Affirmations. Pretty soon after scanning all the Affirmations, you will find yourself attached to a select few. Draw on their power to lift your confidence. Put random statements together. For example, you may feel an affinity for something in Chapter 7 and Chapter 10. Put them together and make that new Affirmation your own. Do you have a favorite superpower word? Throw it in the mix.

- I *Got This* is always useful at any time; you can buy it whenever you choose during the school year and get some kind of value from it? Even though we are introducing affirmations at the middle and high school levels, they will sustain you through college, career and life.

I Got This: Affirmations For Teens to Relieve Stress and Create an Awesome School Year, gives you the strategies to manage overwhelm, master your days and make it through the school year. Superman can be crippled by kryptonite. Wolverine can be cut down by the red muramusa blade. Iron Man's heart could stop beating because of shrapnel. Daredevil can't stand loud noises. Stress can become your kryptonite, your muramusa blade or the too loud noise when you don't know how to manage it. Use the book to learn how to develop your own stress-buster techniques and become more peaceful. Superheroes have awesome tools and pledges. Use *I Got This* as a tool. Let the Affirmations become your own superhero pledges. They will help you gain confidence, visualize accomplishing your goals and embrace the outcome you desire.

FALL

I AM READY FOR ADVENTURE AND SUCCESS

Most schools start the year in the fall. It is a beautiful time of year for learning. The weather is changing from the hot outdoorsy summer to cooler temperatures. It's very picturesque as the green leaves change to beautiful shades of red, magenta, orange, blue, yellow, purple, bronze and brown.

As students, you are ready to absorb the newness of the season fully rested from the rigors of the past semester. You are refreshed. Your teachers are also refreshed and ready to facilitate your learning. Expectations are high on both your part and that of your teachers.

What should you expect in the beginning? All your teachers will give you a syllabus that welcomes you to the process. It will outline their expectations, goals, a pacing guide or timeline that tells you what you will be learning, how long it will take. Added to that, the little speech your teachers give about themselves. Then there are other important tools like textbooks, dictionaries, pens and pencils.

Right away, all your teachers will give you an assessment, a type of quiz that gives them a heads up of your readiness for the new course. It is not a life sentence. They just want to know how much you learned in the lower grade and whether or not you met the benchmarks. What are benchmarks? I see you scratching your head. They are standards or learning goals that measure what you must learn at each grade level. Got it? Yes. I know you understand. Cool.

Let me help you to navigate key ideas this fall semester with these Affirmations. What's that? They are short self-talk passages, declaring your truth that will help you to resolve to hang in there this fall and the rest of the school year. Additionally, you will get the opportunity to spend a week on each topic by writing in your daily journal.

The fall brings lots of new adventures. Have fun!

First Day Blues

SITUATION

All this pushing and shoving, bumping into desks and chairs just to sit in the back of the classroom. No! She didn't just roll her eyes at me. Is that a thing? I feel like I am going to throw up. Finally, I am sitting in front of this teacher who gives me this ten ton packet of paper with "Syllabus and Contracts" sprawled on the front cover for me and my parents to sign. Who is going to read all of this? Who she expects to do all this work?

AFFIRMATION

I am calm. I choose to relax with the students in my class and I easily handle this workload.

Daily Journal

MONDAY

TUESDAY

WEDNESDAY

THURSDAY

FRIDAY

Reflect On

WHAT I DID WELL AND WHAT STILL NEEDS MY ATTENTION

SATURDAY

SUNDAY

I work smart
and I make it happen

COURSE OR ASSIGNMENT NAME	SCORE THIS WEEK	COMPLETE OR INCOMPLETE

2.

Expectations

SITUATION

First Period is in full swing and my teacher is walking around and handing out a sheet of neon pink colored paper with a list of expectations. We are instructed to keep it in the front of our binder at all times because we will be referring to the expectations from time to time. What's wrong with this teacher? I have seven other teachers with their own set of dos and don'ts. All these rules, regulations and routines. How many times is she going to talk about honesty and hard work? We get the point. Get this one! As hard as I work for this teacher, she will take off points for late work and grammar. Really! I won't pass this course for sure. My teacher is setting me up to fail.

AFFIRMATION

I am enthusiastic about this course. Class rules and regulations are cool with me and simple enough to follow. I am capable of turning in my work on time. I am successful in this course and get good grades.

Daily Journal

MONDAY

TUESDAY

WEDNESDAY

THURSDAY

FRIDAY

Reflect On

WHAT I DID WELL AND WHAT STILL NEEDS MY ATTENTION

SATURDAY

SUNDAY

I work smart
and I make it happen

COURSE OR ASSIGNMENT NAME	SCORE THIS WEEK	COMPLETE OR INCOMPLETE

3.

Academic Integrity Is Like Your Thumb Print

SITUATION

I have this paper to do for my History teacher. I just don't get why all my teachers set these big project due dates around the same time? Don't they talk to each other? It is impossible for me to do all this research. Internet to the rescue! I have access to so many research papers online, some are even for sale. Yeah. All I have to do is just cut and paste, put my name on it and call it a day.

AFFIRMATION

This History paper is done well. I know how to research and use information properly. I feel better when I submit my own original work. I respect the work of other researchers and writers. I cite sources and give credit to others. I am honest and trustworthy.

Daily Journal

MONDAY

TUESDAY

WEDNESDAY

THURSDAY

FRIDAY

Reflect On

WHAT I DID WELL AND WHAT STILL NEEDS MY ATTENTION

SATURDAY

SUNDAY

I work smart
and I make it happen

COURSE OR ASSIGNMENT NAME	SCORE THIS WEEK	COMPLETE OR INCOMPLETE

4.

Ask For Help

SITUATION

Reading comprehension has been hard for me. I fail most of my quizzes especially when I try to read on my own. One day, I couldn't take it any longer, climbed up on my chair and yelled: "Is this book on Youtube? Is it a movie?" I wish I could understand everything.

AFFIRMATION

It is okay for me to get help when I need it.
I understand that I have a unique learning style. Every day,
I am improving. I got this!.

Daily Journal

MONDAY

TUESDAY

WEDNESDAY

THURSDAY

FRIDAY

Reflect On

WHAT I DID WELL AND WHAT STILL NEEDS MY ATTENTION

SATURDAY

SUNDAY

I work smart
and I make it happen

COURSE OR ASSIGNMENT NAME	SCORE THIS WEEK	COMPLETE OR INCOMPLETE

5.

Pacing Myself

SITUATION

I am all up in my feelings right now. Another late assignment. There is just not enough time in my day to get all this work done. My grades are dropping like crazy.

AFFIRMATION

I choose to have a good attitude about myself today. I am smart about asking for extra time to complete assignments. I respond confidently to all my assignments because I carefully plan my day. I can do this.

Daily Journal

MONDAY

TUESDAY

WEDNESDAY

THURSDAY

FRIDAY

Reflect On

WHAT I DID WELL AND WHAT STILL NEEDS MY ATTENTION

SATURDAY

SUNDAY

I work smart
and I make it happen

COURSE OR ASSIGNMENT NAME	SCORE THIS WEEK	COMPLETE OR INCOMPLETE

6.

Your First Test

SITUATION

No one dislikes exams like me. When I get awful grades, which is most of the time, I hide them from my peers and turn them face down on my desk. Sometimes, I just crumple and toss them in the garbage. I will never do better in this school.

AFFIRMATION

I boldly face any examination I am given. I accept the grade I receive and use it as my launch pad to improve next time. I appreciate the feedback my teachers give me and I master new skills.

Daily Journal

MONDAY

TUESDAY

WEDNESDAY

THURSDAY

FRIDAY

Reflect On

WHAT I DID WELL AND WHAT STILL NEEDS MY ATTENTION

SATURDAY

SUNDAY

I work smart
and I make it happen

COURSE OR ASSIGNMENT NAME	SCORE THIS WEEK	COMPLETE OR INCOMPLETE

7.

Respect for Students With Special Needs

SITUATION

The students say that something is really wrong with Hector's brain since he had the field hockey accident. They dub him because he can't remember jack. This boy is bad news for our group assignment grade.

AFFIRMATION

I am comfortable with the special needs students in our group. I am mindful of the way I treat my classmates who are different. I choose to be polite. We ace our projects when we collaborate with each other. Every student matters.

Daily Journal

MONDAY

TUESDAY

WEDNESDAY

THURSDAY

FRIDAY

Reflect On

WHAT I DID WELL AND WHAT STILL NEEDS MY ATTENTION

SATURDAY

SUNDAY

I work smart
and I make it happen

COURSE OR ASSIGNMENT NAME	SCORE THIS WEEK	COMPLETE OR INCOMPLETE

8.

Organizing My Life For Any Role I Desire

SITUATION

I really want to become class president. However, I feel like I am doing too much. I am going to way too many club activities. I am chronically late to events, miss important appointments with my peers and school leaders. The bottom fell out the day everything spilled out of my locker onto the hallway floor. I looked like a hoarder. It was embarrassing.

AFFIRMATION

I carefully prioritize my activities. I choose well and still manage to have fun. I show up on time for appointments. I plan my day and get everything done. I am a good role model and student leader.

Daily Journal

MONDAY

TUESDAY

WEDNESDAY

THURSDAY

FRIDAY

Reflect On

WHAT I DID WELL AND WHAT STILL NEEDS MY ATTENTION

SATURDAY

SUNDAY

I work smart
and I make it happen

COURSE OR ASSIGNMENT NAME	SCORE THIS WEEK	COMPLETE OR INCOMPLETE

9.

Question Everything

SITUATION

I don't like to raise my hand in class to ask questions. It's embarrassing. All eyes are on me. Worse, sometimes we are expected to get into groups and ask questions of our peers during the lesson. Suppose I say the wrong thing! I keep losing points because I never ask questions. It's not fair. All my life I was told to "shut up."

AFFIRMATION

I am comfortable asking questions. I feel strong. My curiosity is my greatest strength. It helps me learn quickly, make critical decisions and adapt to change. I speak up.

Daily Journal

MONDAY

TUESDAY

WEDNESDAY

THURSDAY

FRIDAY

Reflect On

WHAT I DID WELL AND WHAT STILL NEEDS MY ATTENTION

SATURDAY

SUNDAY

I work smart
and I make it happen

COURSE OR ASSIGNMENT NAME	SCORE THIS WEEK	COMPLETE OR INCOMPLETE

10.

Independent Study Is A Gift

SITUATION

Lately, it feels unpleasant to be one of the smartest students in my class. I feel drowned out by the bad behavior of some students my teacher, Mr. D calls, 'a bunch of disaffected youth'. They get all the attention. Nothing is left for any other student. I am bored to tears. What's the point in coming? I want more. This school can't help me.

AFFIRMATION

I like that I am intelligent and working with gifted and conscientious students makes my lessons go smoothly. I ask my teacher to assign me an independent project and I feel motivated to go off and work on my own. I take full control of my learning. My knowledge increases when I purposely practice on my own.

30

Daily Journal

MONDAY

TUESDAY

WEDNESDAY

THURSDAY

FRIDAY

Reflect On

WHAT I DID WELL AND WHAT STILL NEEDS MY ATTENTION

SATURDAY

SUNDAY

I work smart
and I make it happen

COURSE OR ASSIGNMENT NAME	SCORE THIS WEEK	COMPLETE OR INCOMPLETE

11.

Vocabulary

SITUATION

I failed the last two vocabulary quizzes. Now my punishment is to write meaningful sentences. Worse, I have to write a poem. That's stupid. People don't use these words in real life.

AFFIRMATION

Words help me express my emotions.
Words help me to communicate well. Learning to spell makes my brain sharper. I learn new words every day. I am proud of myself.

Daily Journal

MONDAY

TUESDAY

WEDNESDAY

THURSDAY

FRIDAY

Reflect On

WHAT I DID WELL AND WHAT STILL NEEDS MY ATTENTION

SATURDAY

SUNDAY

I work smart
and I make it happen

COURSE OR ASSIGNMENT NAME	SCORE THIS WEEK	COMPLETE OR INCOMPLETE

12.

Learning Objectives Are Actually Helpful

SITUATION

Can somebody tell me why some of my teachers put these long complicated state Learning Objectives on the Smartboard every day? They are not written in simple language for students like me. Break it down people! Trying to figure out what my teachers want me to learn on any given day is like rocket science. How am I going to know if I learned what I am supposed to learn?

AFFIRMATION

I am clear about what my teachers need me to know at the end of each lesson. I acknowledge that Learning Objectives are active steps that guide me to answer the aim question and solve problems. I meet my daily objectives in my lessons and assessing my own understanding is easy. I write what I learn. I share with the class what I learn. I got this!.

Daily Journal

MONDAY

TUESDAY

WEDNESDAY

THURSDAY

FRIDAY

Reflect On

WHAT I DID WELL AND WHAT STILL NEEDS MY ATTENTION

SATURDAY

SUNDAY

I work smart
and I make it happen

COURSE OR ASSIGNMENT NAME	SCORE THIS WEEK	COMPLETE OR INCOMPLETE

13.

Working Collaboratively

SITUATION

I like working in my little corner that I carve out for myself in the classroom because I get more done. I hate working in groups because kids nowadays don't know how to focus. The second week in the semester my teacher sends a letter home to my parents about me refusing to work with the other kids. He claims they depend on my input. This makes no sense when all they do is talk about everything but the lesson. Now I'm grounded. I lost my cellphone privilege.

AFFIRMATION

I easily work with others. I have the skill to help the group maintain focus. I listen carefully and respect other students' opinions. I like when we ask each other questions about the lesson. It helps me see the problem from different viewpoints. Everybody's ideas enrich the group. I can do this.

Daily Journal

MONDAY

TUESDAY

WEDNESDAY

THURSDAY

FRIDAY

Reflect On

WHAT I DID WELL AND WHAT STILL NEEDS MY ATTENTION

SATURDAY

SUNDAY

I work smart
and I make it happen

COURSE OR ASSIGNMENT NAME	SCORE THIS WEEK	COMPLETE OR INCOMPLETE

14.

Learning Outcomes Are Just a List of Your Superpowers

SITUATION

Sometimes when my teacher sets goals for a lesson, I get so frustrated. There are just too many steps to consider for the task. Too much to think about in one lesson. On top of that, I have to prove that I learned something.

AFFIRMATION

I feel inspired by this lesson. I plan every step I need to take. I meet the goals of the lesson and learning is easier. Now, I am a deep thinker. I am a heroic private eye. I am a problem solver. I am able to remember key ideas. I am successful in this lesson. I have superpowers.
I do this well!.

Daily Journal

MONDAY

TUESDAY

WEDNESDAY

THURSDAY

FRIDAY

Reflect On

WHAT I DID WELL AND WHAT STILL NEEDS MY ATTENTION

SATURDAY

SUNDAY

I work smart
and I make it happen

COURSE OR ASSIGNMENT NAME	SCORE THIS WEEK	COMPLETE OR INCOMPLETE

WINTER

Exploring Theories, Themes and Strategies

A magical time of the year!

Winter gets freezing cold in some parts of the world and tends to be breezy and chilly in other areas. The beautiful fall leaves have burned off, leaving the trees bare. The winter solstice has set in as a section of the earth slants away from the sun. No other time of the year is more festive than the end of year celebrations. It's camera! Lights! Action! The winter season at school demands the same.

Face to face interactions begin to diminish and loneliness and sadness may creep. It is time to go inward. That means you must find the inner strength to really motivate yourself to stay on top of coursework. You need to stay alert. Don't be scared. It is the season to become aware of your physical and emotional health. Get involved in school activities.

You can expect that your teacher will be pushing you to complete important assignments to make you ready for midyear examinations. There will be frequent reviews. Be prepared to study harder. Some teachers will give you assignments that require you to be outdoors in the winter; whether spending time at the public library or museum. You should be working collaboratively on your first major project. It's also time to start assembling your portfolio. What's a portfolio? It is a binder that you compile with your best work, certificates of accomplishments and kudos for presentation at the end of the school year. Your teacher will give you a guideline to follow.

Sounds like a lot is going on here! It just means you are required to be organized. This book will help but don't hesitate to ask your parents and teachers for pointers. The good thing is that you have a winter break; much needed time off to take a deep breath and get some rest. Remember to have some fun!

15.

Self-Care

SITUATION

I dread cold and flu season. I get very little sleep. Nothing comes in and out of my brain easily. I am scared to touch anyone or anything. Who knows what people have? I am stressed to the max.

AFFIRMATION

I take care of myself. I anticipate flu season and feeding my body with healthy foods makes me sleep better. When I exercise my body, I am more energetic, my memory improves, I can manage my stress and I have a great attitude. I am a healthy student.

Daily Journal

MONDAY

TUESDAY

WEDNESDAY

THURSDAY

FRIDAY

Reflect On

WHAT I DID WELL AND WHAT STILL NEEDS MY ATTENTION

SATURDAY

SUNDAY

I work smart
and I make it happen

COURSE OR ASSIGNMENT NAME	SCORE THIS WEEK	COMPLETE OR INCOMPLETE

16.

Clubs Are A Great Way to Learn and Make Friends

SITUATION

I met with my counselor today to plan my courses and activities for next semester. She expressed concern that I had not joined any clubs. Well, what she didn't know is that I messed up last semester by hanging out with my friends after school and got home late way too many times. I have to build up courage to ask my parents who are worried sick about my safety in the winter months when it's darker. I really want to join the chess club this year.

AFFIRMATION

Joining the chess club opens me up to think strategically, problem solve and be more focused. I make new friends who share similar values for success in school. When I am with my peers, I make good decisions. I coolly demonstrate to my parents that I am aware of my surroundings, responsible and have self-control. I am smarter.

Daily Journal

MONDAY

TUESDAY

WEDNESDAY

THURSDAY

FRIDAY

Reflect On

WHAT I DID WELL AND WHAT STILL NEEDS MY ATTENTION

SATURDAY

SUNDAY

I work smart
and I make it happen

COURSE OR ASSIGNMENT NAME	SCORE THIS WEEK	COMPLETE OR INCOMPLETE

17.

Ramp up Study Habits

SITUATION

My friends make me happy and it's really fun to Facetime with them all day. Sometimes we Facetime when we are sitting beside each other. It's hilarious. Guess what? Everything else is depressing. I suck at pop quizzes. I am clueless how to fix this and I want good grades.

AFFIRMATION

My friends are important to my social and emotional well-being. I use my time with them wisely. I invite my friends to study with me on Facetime in the evenings after school. We have fun and I easily remember what we study. I give myself permission to get good grades.
I am the master of my time!.

Daily Journal

MONDAY

TUESDAY

WEDNESDAY

THURSDAY

FRIDAY

Reflect On

WHAT I DID WELL AND WHAT STILL NEEDS MY ATTENTION

SATURDAY

SUNDAY

I work smart
and I make it happen

COURSE OR ASSIGNMENT NAME	SCORE THIS WEEK	COMPLETE OR INCOMPLETE

18.

Winter Recital Blues

SITUATION

Singing in a play is the weirdest thing to me. Why can't the actors just dialog with each other? They want people to sound stupid when they are singing. Worse, they want us to dance while we are singing. Really? I feel really self-conscious. What's with the crowd! There are way too many people working on this show.

AFFIRMATION

Learning the dialog, the dance steps and the music is fun. All the students have a superpower on stage. I am a superpower when I am working with other students to act, sing, dance, make costumes, do set design and lighting. Music is fun. My friends are in the band, jump around on stage and rock out anyway. I can do it.

Daily Journal

MONDAY

TUESDAY

WEDNESDAY

THURSDAY

FRIDAY

Reflect On

WHAT I DID WELL AND WHAT STILL NEEDS MY ATTENTION

SATURDAY

SUNDAY

I work smart
and I make it happen

COURSE OR ASSIGNMENT NAME	SCORE THIS WEEK	COMPLETE OR INCOMPLETE

19.

O Algebra, O Algebra, Such Happiness You Bring Me

SITUATION

Why am I doing so many algebra sections? This is such a horrible course. The Xs and Ys don't make sense. Plus, you have to remember all these stupid rules and formulas. We don't use that stuff in real life. I am going to become an actor and for the life of me I can't understand why I need algebra. Actors don't need algebra to make it on Broadway or in Hollywood. Save me!

AFFIRMATION

Doing Algebra helps me develop analytical skills, my ability to reason and solve complex problems. All careers need these analytical superpowers. I use my creativity and acting skills to help me create rap, spoken word, mnemonics, silly song or skit to memorize the rules and formulas in Algebra. I teach my peers these memorization skills. I am acing Algebra!

Daily Journal

MONDAY

TUESDAY

WEDNESDAY

THURSDAY

FRIDAY

Reflect On

WHAT I DID WELL AND WHAT STILL NEEDS MY ATTENTION

SATURDAY

SUNDAY

I work smart
and I make it happen

COURSE OR ASSIGNMENT NAME	SCORE THIS WEEK	COMPLETE OR INCOMPLETE

20.

Feelings About HIV and AIDS

SITUATION

My bestie confided in me in Middle School that she is living with HIV, which she acquired from her mother at birth. Somehow word got out about her diagnosis and the children avoid her and sometimes they say mean things to her. She feels isolated and alone most of the times. It hurts my heart to see her that way and I feel helpless.

AFFIRMATION

I am becoming more aware that I too can play my part in helping to get rid of the stigmas associated with HIV and AIDS. I care deeply about my bestie who is getting the help she needs to live healthy and be treated as an equal in our school community. I volunteer my time to the HIV and AIDS Awareness program in my school. I help to educate others about the disease. I am curious to discover ways to cure this disease. I am a champion for our health.

Daily Journal

MONDAY

TUESDAY

WEDNESDAY

THURSDAY

FRIDAY

Reflect On

WHAT I DID WELL AND WHAT STILL NEEDS MY ATTENTION

SATURDAY

SUNDAY

I work smart
and I make it happen

COURSE OR ASSIGNMENT NAME	SCORE THIS WEEK	COMPLETE OR INCOMPLETE

21.

One-on-One with
my teacher is not happening

SITUATION

From Day One, I have this hunch that Mr. Tucker does not like a bone in my body. Somehow, he finds a way to squeeze into every lesson an awful tale of his holiday in Africa. Then he stares me down, so creepy, like he dares me to just open my African mouth and say something. I don't understand gonadotropic—something—something response. Can I get help? No. Unfortunately my teacher is racist. It's not going to be a good conversation.

AFFIRMATION

I know who I am. I am proud of my heritage. I am strong. I am worthy. I access an abundance of information in the school's online database and the public library. I easily meet with my teacher and get the help I need.

Daily Journal

MONDAY

TUESDAY

WEDNESDAY

THURSDAY

FRIDAY

Reflect On

WHAT I DID WELL AND WHAT STILL NEEDS MY ATTENTION

SATURDAY

SUNDAY

I work smart
and I make it happen

COURSE OR ASSIGNMENT NAME	SCORE THIS WEEK	COMPLETE OR INCOMPLETE

My Quiet Space

SITUATION

My brother and sister are constantly fighting and quarrelling over who moved what, who took what, who did what. The sirens scream through the neighborhood every hour on the hour. I can't find a place to think and just be myself.

AFFIRMATION

In this moment, I embrace stillness, knowing that my siblings are discovering who they are. I create my quiet space anywhere to be with my thoughts.
In this space, I am who I am.

Daily Journal

MONDAY

TUESDAY

WEDNESDAY

THURSDAY

FRIDAY

Reflect On

WHAT I DID WELL AND WHAT STILL NEEDS MY ATTENTION

SATURDAY

SUNDAY

I work smart
and I make it happen

COURSE OR ASSIGNMENT NAME	SCORE THIS WEEK	COMPLETE OR INCOMPLETE

23.

My Portfolio is Me Improving Every Day

SITUATION

Of all the expectations my teacher talks about at the beginning of the school year, this is the one that's most scary: the ridiculous portfolio. Who likes that? My ELA teacher is just too extra. Trying to keep most of my work together to show my growth is getting on my last nerve. How is looking at my past work going to help me? Does she even know that I live in a homeless shelter? OMG. I've got bigger problems.

AFFIRMATION

My portfolio keeps me organized. Everything is in one place. My graded assignments from the lowest to the highest, project logs, lessons, certificates of achievement and my written help me strategize and fix problems. My portfolio reflects that I am becoming a better scholar. I feel good that that I am planning for the future and improving my situation. I am moving from homeless shelter to "A" for awesome!

Daily Journal

MONDAY

TUESDAY

WEDNESDAY

THURSDAY

FRIDAY

Reflect On

WHAT I DID WELL AND WHAT STILL NEEDS MY ATTENTION

SATURDAY

SUNDAY

I work smart
and I make it happen

COURSE OR ASSIGNMENT NAME	SCORE THIS WEEK	COMPLETE OR INCOMPLETE

24.

Money, Finance and Me

SITUATION

Sometimes, when I listen to my parents talk about not having enough money to support the family, I swear we are the poorest on the planet. It is distressing. I didn't ask them to have me when they have no money. Why are they complaining? They are the adults. It's so embarrassing. There are days I just cannot imagine success in my world.

AFFIRMATION

I am valuable. I am enough. I am thankful to my parents for all they do. I am becoming focused and smart about money. I treat my grade point average like my credit score. I take more AP courses and earn a grade of 4 or 5 to pay for the most cost-effective college and save my family borrowing money. My saving superpower is on fire. My success is unfolding right now.

Daily Journal

MONDAY

TUESDAY

WEDNESDAY

THURSDAY

FRIDAY

Reflect On

WHAT I DID WELL AND WHAT STILL NEEDS MY ATTENTION

SATURDAY

SUNDAY

I work smart
and I make it happen

COURSE OR ASSIGNMENT NAME	SCORE THIS WEEK	COMPLETE OR INCOMPLETE

25.

Looking After My Siblings

SITUATION

Eight courses. Eight winter break assignments and I am exhausted. I have to babysit my three younger brothers, cook for them, help them with their winter assignments, keep them from wrecking the house and get them ready for bed. They are ridiculously noisy and they leave their stupid toys everywhere. Mom is picking up extra break-back holiday hours to take care of us and doesn't come home until after midnight. Then, I get to work on my eight assignments into the wee hours of the morning and fall asleep on the table. Who takes care of me?

AFFIRMATION

I love my mom and my brothers. I am energized. I effortlessly plan my day's activities. I like showing my brothers how to be helpful and I give them chores. I create nap time for them and for myself so we can all rest. I show gratitude to my mother for her hard work and celebrate all of our accomplishments. Winter recess is wonderful because I still have fun and spend time with my imagination. I practice mindfulness. I am fine.

Daily Journal

MONDAY

TUESDAY

WEDNESDAY

THURSDAY

FRIDAY

Reflect On

WHAT I DID WELL AND WHAT STILL NEEDS MY ATTENTION

SATURDAY

SUNDAY

I work smart
and I make it happen

COURSE OR ASSIGNMENT NAME	SCORE THIS WEEK	COMPLETE OR INCOMPLETE

26.

Staying Curious About Science

SITUATION

Ever since I heard about the students who got badly burned in the lab at school, I have been petrified about science experiments. Now, I have missed way too many lab hours to pass this course. If this is what science is all about, I can live without it for real.

AFFIRMATION

I follow the lab guidelines. I am careful about conducting experiments in the lab and spending quality time completing my labs and passing this course is worth the effort. Every day I become more mindful that science is all around me from the moment I take my first morning breath, to linking with my friends on my cellphone to buying my lunch in the cafeteria. When I engage in science, I transform into an intrepid private investigator in search of evidence to support the hypothesis. Science teaches me how to solve problems, make decisions and come up with creative ways to function better in the world. Understanding science motivates me to learn other subjects. Science is fun to explore.

Daily Journal

MONDAY

TUESDAY

WEDNESDAY

THURSDAY

FRIDAY

Reflect On

WHAT I DID WELL AND WHAT STILL NEEDS MY ATTENTION

SATURDAY

SUNDAY

I work smart
and I make it happen

COURSE OR ASSIGNMENT NAME	SCORE THIS WEEK	COMPLETE OR INCOMPLETE

MIDYEAR REFLECTION

Journal Entry Date: __/__/__

Write a Journal entry about some key steps you have taken to this midpoint in order to grow as a student and a human being. Write freely about that which interests you, still challenges you and what you enjoy.

_____

_____

_____

_____

_____

_____

_____

_____

_____

_____

_____

_____

_____

SPRING

I am Learning New Things

O the joys of spring!

It has been raining steadily and in some parts, the snow has melted. There is new life. Trees and plants are flowering again, the birds have returned and you are ready to go outdoors.

Some of you have complained that you get stressed out during this period. No matter how hard you try, you find it difficult to balance academics with extracurricular activities. After all, students need to be well rounded, and activities on and off campus look good on your college application.

One of the dangers with the spring is that students tend to become more inclined to socialize. Temperatures are rising and they are warming up to pleasure. They want to spend less time in the classroom. Seniors in particular, are tempted to skip class because they left college planning for the last. Not a good idea! Oftentimes, they have fewer classes and in some cases, lethargy sets in. Anxiety about graduation consumes them.

Your teachers have pulled out all the stops to prepare you and therefore, expect you to succeed. They carefully take you through the paces with regular reviews and mock exams. The spring is important for practice and test taking. This will ensure that you are ready to sit those State and College Board examinations. The stakes are high.

What to do? It is time to pay attention to your mental health. Revisit your calendar of events and strike a balance between fun and school work. Spend time with friends. What better way than in study groups. Attend the school play. Make time to celebrate you! Remember, you get to spend time with family on spring break. Make every moment count. Have fun!

27.

Video Game Wins and GPA Scores

SITUATION

I feel so violated right now. When I came home from school this afternoon, my dad had removed the door to my bedroom. It's evil. My television was gone. No more video games. I am good at video games! The school called. My report card was terrible. I failed chemistry, biology and English Language Arts and I want to go to college and work in computer gaming. Even so, he didn't have to take my door off. There's no privacy in this house and it's my room.

AFFIRMATION

I accept that actions have consequences. Gaming is cool and I use my gaming strategies to memorize the human body, chemical formulas and other science material. It's easy. I am discovering that gaming is storytelling just like Shakespeare's Macbeth and Lord of the Flies. I am paying attention. It is my duty to act responsibly when it comes to my school work. Putting my all into earning good grades and improving my GPA from the ninth grade onward is my priority. I am going to college. I accomplish anything I focus on.

Daily Journal

MONDAY

TUESDAY

WEDNESDAY

THURSDAY

FRIDAY

Reflect On

WHAT I DID WELL AND WHAT STILL NEEDS MY ATTENTION

SATURDAY

SUNDAY

*I work smart
and I make it happen*

COURSE OR ASSIGNMENT NAME	SCORE THIS WEEK	COMPLETE OR INCOMPLETE

28.

How Do I Feel About College

SITUATION

I'm feeling so much pressure from my parents and my teachers, right now, I am going to explode. They are a tag team, my worst nightmare. My parents did not even go to college and they are making it, so what's the major hype? College is not for everybody.

AFFIRMATION

I like that my parents understand the value of a college education and are teaching me. I enjoy our debates. I do my own research to see how college prepares students for the work world. I am being guided to think about my career and I take courses that I need to get my diploma. I visit the college center at my school and read all I can about financial aid, programs and college tours. Going to college gives me more time to make the right decision about my many possible careers, even fun side gigs. College is definitely in my future.

Daily Journal

MONDAY

TUESDAY

WEDNESDAY

THURSDAY

FRIDAY

Reflect On

WHAT I DID WELL AND WHAT STILL NEEDS MY ATTENTION

SATURDAY

SUNDAY

I work smart
and I make it happen

COURSE OR ASSIGNMENT NAME	SCORE THIS WEEK	COMPLETE OR INCOMPLETE

29.

My Emotional Health

SITUATION

These two boys and this girl who sit in front of me turn around in their seats and torture me every day. They call me a sissy, a bulla, a fish. They don't know anything about me but they get the rest of the class to join them in laughing at me. I beg my teacher to move me but he thinks I am the problem, I need to toughen up, I am too sensitive. Some days, I feel like the world is closing in on me, I just want to give up. I hate this school.

AFFIRMATION

I recognize the tactics of bullies and I reach for the strength inside of me to cope. I call on my superpower Affirmations. Quietly saying my Affirmations and my superpower word give me strength and resilience. I am comfortable with myself. I am strong. I see friendly smiles coming from some of my peers. I am protected by caring adults. I know how to be safe. I am worthy. I am perfect, whole and complete.

Daily Journal

MONDAY

TUESDAY

WEDNESDAY

THURSDAY

FRIDAY

Reflect On

SATURDAY

SUNDAY

I work smart
and I make it happen

COURSE OR ASSIGNMENT NAME	SCORE THIS WEEK	COMPLETE OR INCOMPLETE

30.

Appreciating The Language Of Poetry

SITUATION

When I was in elementary school, I learned rhyming poetry. It was fun. Now I am in high school and I am bombarded with poetry that totally makes no sense. I just can't understand this old English stuff. Nobody talks like that. It's irrelevant. My literature teacher gets so animated about classical poetry. "It will show up again on your state exams and in college so better get it right." I'm nauseated. Who cares?

AFFIRMATION

I am open to experience the complexity and simplicity of poetry. I'm learning from the old poets. Rappers are poets. They rhyme and so can I. I accept that people all around the world do poetry. Poetry is my way of using language to express my feelings. April is poetry month and I get to perform anything at the Poetry Slam; free verse, rhyme schemes, iambic pentameter. I am a poet with my bass and drums. I feel free.

Daily Journal

MONDAY

TUESDAY

WEDNESDAY

THURSDAY

FRIDAY

Reflect On

WHAT I DID WELL AND WHAT STILL NEEDS MY ATTENTION

SATURDAY

SUNDAY

I work smart
and I make it happen

COURSE OR ASSIGNMENT NAME	SCORE THIS WEEK	COMPLETE OR INCOMPLETE

31.

Damage Control

SITUATION

It is the heights of spring and I'm still flustered by routines in this school. I despise sudden change. I get cranky and disoriented with classroom changes, schedule changes and when a new teacher takes over mid-session. Why can't the original teacher stay in the classroom for the whole semester? It's ridiculous!

I understand that life happens. My teachers are human beings. I have a good attitude about routine change in my own life, in the classroom, in Nature, the car breaking down, food running out at home. It's an adventure. I use the app on my phone to alert me about changes and timekeeping. I use my Affirmations when there are changes and they keep me calm.

Daily Journal

MONDAY

TUESDAY

WEDNESDAY

THURSDAY

FRIDAY

Reflect On

WHAT I DID WELL AND WHAT STILL NEEDS MY ATTENTION

SATURDAY

SUNDAY

I work smart
and I make it happen

COURSE OR ASSIGNMENT NAME	SCORE THIS WEEK	COMPLETE OR INCOMPLETE

32.

Research Paper

SITUATION

So I get this list of topics from my teacher. I need to choose one for my research paper. I don't like his suggestions. They are not interesting. I have wasted so much time trying to convince my teacher to let me come up with my own topic. It is futile! I can write what I already know: my day at the football or hockey game. I know those things already. They build morals and character. How is my idea a problem?

AFFIRMATION

I work well with others. I practice integrity. I give myself the go-ahead to follow all the guidelines for my research paper. I meet all deadlines in the process. I realize how much passion and interest I have in learning something new. I am one of the librarian's frequent researchers and I get a lot of help. I achieve.

Daily Journal

MONDAY

TUESDAY

WEDNESDAY

THURSDAY

FRIDAY

Reflect On

WHAT I DID WELL AND WHAT STILL NEEDS MY ATTENTION

SATURDAY

SUNDAY

I work smart
and I make it happen

COURSE OR ASSIGNMENT NAME	SCORE THIS WEEK	COMPLETE OR INCOMPLETE

33.

Revitalize Your Life on Spring Break

SITUATION

I have been training for the Outdoor Track and Field Championships coming up in early June. Between the academic demands on my headspace and track practice—I feel sluggish and tired. My coach is like a Pitbull on steroids who is tracking my academic progress and behavior in my other classes, ready to kick me off the team if I mess up. Spring break cannot come soon enough.

AFFIRMATION

I use this much deserved holiday to sleep and have fun. This break restores me to better mental and physical health so I am successful learning and competing. I spend most of the time with my friends and family traveling and doing fun activities. I negotiate nap time with my parents during the day and I also sleep for at least 8 hours at night. This holiday, I take full responsibility for my own vitality and happiness.

Daily Journal

MONDAY

TUESDAY

WEDNESDAY

THURSDAY

FRIDAY

Reflect On

WHAT I DID WELL AND WHAT STILL NEEDS MY ATTENTION

SATURDAY

SUNDAY

I work smart
and I make it happen

COURSE OR ASSIGNMENT NAME	SCORE THIS WEEK	COMPLETE OR INCOMPLETE

34.

Is This on The Test?

SITUATION

As many pop quizzes and other assessments that I do, somehow this school thinks I need to practice until I drop. You know who is in on this craziness—my parents. They don't understand how stressful it is. Sometimes I just sit there and look at the multiple choice test. I tell myself there are just some theories I will not get.

AFFIRMATION

I identify areas that I master and those areas where I improve. I know I am supported all the way and research ways to understand and memorize complex theories. I listen to myself breathing deeply and quietly say my Affirmations on mock exam day. I am calm. I am a winner.

Daily Journal

MONDAY

TUESDAY

WEDNESDAY

THURSDAY

FRIDAY

Reflect On

WHAT I DID WELL AND WHAT STILL NEEDS MY ATTENTION

SATURDAY

SUNDAY

I work smart
and I make it happen

COURSE OR ASSIGNMENT NAME	SCORE THIS WEEK	COMPLETE OR INCOMPLETE

35.

Acing the State and Final Exams

SITUATION

It is state and final exam season and skill and drills have left me seriously doubtful and cynical about the purpose for my education. First there are the petty teachers who take off points for everything. Then there are those who mark on the curve. Not to be outdone are the ones who have favorites. I can't remember anything. The school is so lame. They don't even have enough computers for research and practice. The teachers don't have enough resources to help me either. No textbooks. No notebooks. My parents don't have it! Forget passing exams in these conditions. Did I say I can't remember anything? Too stressful!

AFFIRMATION

I am prepared. I know how I need to conduct myself in this exam setting. I close my eyes and take deep breaths. I remember everything. I trust in my abilities to respond to every question in the way I was taught and how I studied. I am ready to have fun on my exams. I am confident.
I am smart. I got this!.

Daily Journal

MONDAY

TUESDAY

WEDNESDAY

THURSDAY

FRIDAY

Reflect On

WHAT I DID WELL AND WHAT STILL NEEDS MY ATTENTION

SATURDAY

SUNDAY

I work smart
and I make it happen

COURSE OR ASSIGNMENT NAME	SCORE THIS WEEK	COMPLETE OR INCOMPLETE

36.

Life Skills Are
The Essence of All My Learning

SITUATION

Sometimes I sit and contemplate the meaning of life and whether or not my academic paper-learning has prepared me to function after graduation. What skills did I develop to earn money, pay my bills, travel with my friends and solve real-world challenges? This is lame.

AFFIRMATION

I have lots of examples and role models around me. I efficiently use the skills I learn from studying academic subjects to solve real-world problems. I make good decisions. I collaborate well in group settings. I plan and manage my time well. I think critically. I communicate clearly with my peers. I successfully handle money matters wisely. I intentionally take care of my body and mind. I am taking charge of my life.

Daily Journal

MONDAY

TUESDAY

WEDNESDAY

THURSDAY

FRIDAY

Reflect On

WHAT I DID WELL AND WHAT STILL NEEDS MY ATTENTION

SATURDAY

SUNDAY

I work smart
and I make it happen

COURSE OR ASSIGNMENT NAME	SCORE THIS WEEK	COMPLETE OR INCOMPLETE

SUMMER

A Second Chance to Get it Right

It is hot. Occasional rain and heavy winds characterize this fireworks season. Summer is the beach-lover's delight. Families who live in colder climates try to make their way to tropical climates where they have the sun on their faces. There is plenty of time to relax and have fun, read, surf, play volleyball, tennis or board games. That's how it is for some folks while others have to attend summer school for four out of the ten-week holiday. This is a second chance to make up for low grades earned during the fall, winter or spring sessions.

If this is your situation, then you can either attend the summer program at your school or one nearby where make-up courses are offered. Today, there are learning cafes where you have access to online technology and myriad courses from which to choose. You get the opportunity to reinforce what you learned earlier in the school year. You will be able to retain the information so you can build on the knowledge in the coming school year. Moreover, you get to learn new concepts and ideas, make new friends and improve your social skills.

Have you ever wondered about the benefits of spending time in the sun? I mean safe time—not too much exposure to the UV rays. Well, you get much needed natural Vitamin D to help you build healthy bones and strengthen your immune system. This helps to prevent colds and flus for a healthy return to school in the fall. Do your parents do this? Take care of your body, balance healthy eating with pigging out, and play. Pay attention to skin breakouts. Are they a sign to manage your sugar intake?

One of the downsides to having too much time on your hands during the summer is the likelihood that some teenagers may become reckless and indulge in underage drinking. This can be detrimental to your health, affect you getting scholarships for college and it could ruin your career. Don't do it.

Although summer is loud and social, you will need to carve out some time to regroup before school reopens. Start preparing your new school clothes, school backpack and materials you will need. Go online and find ways to help your parents save money on your school supplies. They will thank you for it and you will be learning about budgeting and personal finance. Find a way to make fun-times a learning opportunity. This way, you will be sharp and ready for new knowledge in the fall. You can do it!

37.

Second Chance to
Review, Redo, Refine

SITUATION

I worked as hard as I could but I didn't get the grades. The only alternative is to attend summer school. This is my second chance to improve on those subjects I struggled with and failed. I would rather be playing online power games with other teens around the world.

AFFIRMATION

I gladly accept a second chance to review, redo, refine. I am lucky. Summer school is only six weeks of my time and I use it well knowing I am going to have so much fun later. I already know some of the material. I capably focus on those challenging concepts that need my attention. I ace summer school.

Daily Journal

MONDAY

TUESDAY

WEDNESDAY

THURSDAY

FRIDAY

Reflect On

WHAT I DID WELL AND WHAT STILL NEEDS MY ATTENTION

SATURDAY

SUNDAY

I work smart
and I make it happen

COURSE OR ASSIGNMENT NAME	SCORE THIS WEEK	COMPLETE OR INCOMPLETE

38.

Museums Bring Cultures Together

SITUATION

It is sad we do not have a museum within a hundred miles of the hood. Museum is for rich people. My friends think we would look like wannabees so we don't go.

AFFIRMATION

Museums are for everyone. I encourage my peers to visit museums. I have fun exploring museums on my own. I value the rich cultural heritage and treasures of my ancestors and elders. I want to know the people in my family tree. I recognize the wealth of knowledge, history and creativity that is present in my own community. I collect artifacts and create a museum in our school that tells our stories.

Daily Journal

MONDAY

TUESDAY

WEDNESDAY

THURSDAY

FRIDAY

Reflect On

WHAT I DID WELL AND WHAT STILL NEEDS MY ATTENTION

SATURDAY

SUNDAY

I work smart
and I make it happen

COURSE OR ASSIGNMENT NAME	SCORE THIS WEEK	COMPLETE OR INCOMPLETE

39.

Reading for Pleasure and Reading for Life

SITUATION

I have never read a full novel or play. Most of my teachers believe teenagers have the attention span of a goldfish. I think it's true except I pay attention to other things. Anyway, we only need to read short excerpts to pass standardized state exams.

AFFIRMATION

At the library, I am finding stories that are exciting and that hold my attention. The librarian helps me choose from action, horror, crime, thrillers, war stories, love stories. There are stories for me. I know what I like now. I expand my knowledge about the world when I read. It's an easy way to learn about far away cultures. I have an adventure exploring literature. I am learning the techniques of complex literary, technical and academic writing. I love reading.

Daily Journal

MONDAY

TUESDAY

WEDNESDAY

THURSDAY

FRIDAY

Reflect On

WHAT I DID WELL AND WHAT STILL NEEDS MY ATTENTION

SATURDAY

SUNDAY

I work smart
and I make it happen

COURSE OR ASSIGNMENT NAME	SCORE THIS WEEK	COMPLETE OR INCOMPLETE

40.

Family and Teacher Working Together for My Success

SITUATION

"Listen here child, I send you to school for the teacher to teach you and for you to learn. That is all I ask you to do. I don't have the time to follow after your teacher to find out how you are doing or not doing." That's how my mother sounds when she comes home and I tell her she needs to come with me to meet my teachers on Parent-Teacher Night. I feel like a castaway.

AFFIRMATION

I am grateful that my parents make the effort to meet with my teachers to plan for my success. I am motivated and work even harder. I am learning that I need to show them I am grateful. I understand my mom is human and can get stressed out. I am improving my relationship with my mom. I promise her and my teachers I can work smart. We got this!

Daily Journal

MONDAY

TUESDAY

WEDNESDAY

THURSDAY

FRIDAY

Reflect On

WHAT I DID WELL AND WHAT STILL NEEDS MY ATTENTION

SATURDAY

SUNDAY

I work smart
and I make it happen

COURSE OR ASSIGNMENT NAME	SCORE THIS WEEK	COMPLETE OR INCOMPLETE

41.

Give Myself
a Pat on the Back

SITUATION

It is hard to feel good about myself when I am surrounded by haters and Debbie Downers. I don't want to be different!

AFFIRMATION

I am proud of myself. I give myself a standing ovation for my perseverance and smart work ethic. I am a beautiful person inside and out and I attract brilliant and wonderful friends. I am safe. I accept who I am.

Daily Journal

MONDAY

TUESDAY

WEDNESDAY

THURSDAY

FRIDAY

Reflect On

WHAT I DID WELL AND WHAT STILL NEEDS MY ATTENTION

SATURDAY

SUNDAY

I work smart
and I make it happen

COURSE OR ASSIGNMENT NAME	SCORE THIS WEEK	COMPLETE OR INCOMPLETE

Physical Education is Health Education

SITUATION

I am so self-conscious about my unattractive body. I am failing Physical Education class because I refuse to change into my P.E. uniform and humiliate myself in front of all these mean kids. My teacher takes off points every time I don't wear my P.E. uniform. I am doing exceptionally well in my other courses but this situation makes me cry myself to sleep.

AFFIRMATION

I am strong. This body I am in is the perfect one for me. When I take care of my body with healthy nutrition and rest, I feel good about my appearance. I am ready to participate in Physical Education class. I take responsibility for my Phys. Ed. credits because they impact my GPA and my diploma. I am thankful for Phys. Ed. at school because it helps me keep healthy.

Daily Journal

MONDAY

TUESDAY

WEDNESDAY

THURSDAY

FRIDAY

Reflect On

WHAT I DID WELL AND WHAT STILL NEEDS MY ATTENTION

SATURDAY

SUNDAY

I work smart
and I make it happen

COURSE OR ASSIGNMENT NAME	SCORE THIS WEEK	COMPLETE OR INCOMPLETE

43.

Moral Values and Compassion

SITUATION

Not many of my peers are aware of the high number of homeless students in this school. When my mom and dad lost their jobs and we became homeless, I went without a bath for several days as we were not allowed in the bathroom at the McDonalds in my area. We were literally living under the highway. I thought of cleaning up in the school bathroom but I didn't want anyone to see me. I didn't think I smelled but my peers and teachers avoided me. I would never want to feel this way again. It was embarrassing. Finally getting beds at the local shelter made the difference until we got back on our feet. Now the local shelter will close because of lack of funds and volunteers.

AFFIRMATION

I thoughtfully commit to helping a cause in my community. I feel fulfilled when I am serving others. I feel good when I collaborate with adults on projects I find interesting. I get Community Service Credit towards my diploma and colleges. I am a useful member of my community.

Daily Journal

MONDAY

TUESDAY

WEDNESDAY

THURSDAY

FRIDAY

Reflect On

WHAT I DID WELL AND WHAT STILL NEEDS MY ATTENTION

SATURDAY

SUNDAY

I work smart
and I make it happen

COURSE OR ASSIGNMENT NAME	SCORE THIS WEEK	COMPLETE OR INCOMPLETE

END OF YEAR REFLECTION

Journal Entry Date: __/__/__

Write freely about your experience as a student this year. How has the learning process helped you to understand who you are and where you hope to be years from now? What interests you, still challenges you and brings you happiness?

_____

_____

_____

_____

_____

_____

_____

_____

_____

_____

_____

_____

_____

_____

NEED MORE
QUESTIONS ANSWERED?

Bullying	https://www.stopbullying.gov/ (National)
	The Brave Line (Local, New York) (212) 709-3222 (Support & Resources)
Child Abuse Hotline	(800) 4-A-CHILD (800) 422-4453)
Child Find of America	(800) I-AM-LOST (800) 426-5678
Civil Rights	Telephone: (800) 421-3481 FAX: (202) 453-6012; TDD: (800) 877-8339 Email: OCR@ed.gov
LGBT National Help Center	888-843-4564 Main 800-246-7743 Youth Line 888-234-7243 Senior
National Domestic Violence Hotline	(800) 799-SAFE (800) 799-7233 TTY (800) 787-3224 Deaf Persons Video Access: (206) 518-9361 https://www.thehotline.org/
National Emergency	911
National Institute of Mental Health	(866) 615-6464 http://www.nimh.nih.gov/index.shtml
National Parent Helpline National Runaway Safeline	(855) 4A PARENT (855) 427-2736) Phone: 800-RUNAWAY (800) 786-2929
National Suicide Prevention Lifeline	(800) 273-TALK (800) 273-8255 TTY (800) 799.-4TTY (800) 799-4889

Rape, Abuse and Incest National Network (RAINN)	(800) 656-HOPE (800) 656-4673
Substance Abuse and Mental Health Services Administration (SAMHSA)	(800) 662-HELP (800) 662-4357 https://www.samhsa.gov/https://www.samhsa.gov/

ACKNOWLEDGEMENTS

There are just so many people to thank for getting this book in your hands. First, let me thank my students for insisting that I write this book for them because I had written one for their parents.

Thanks to Faith Nelson of Watercourse LLC for book development, concept, strategic planning and encouraging me to source Jamaya for editing. I did just that and the results are great.

Thanks to fifteen year old Kyle to whom this book is dedicated and who got me inspired to get this first book in the series, From A Teacher to Students ready for the 2019-2020 school year.

Thanks to Janet Whyte, teacher extraordinaire, for our many summers collaborating on our 180 lesson plans for the year.

Thanks to the Sisal team for pulling out every stop to get this book ready for the summer release.

Thanks to my daughter and granddaughter for being my rock and support system.

Enjoy this book and feel free to write me about anything that puzzles, interests, annoys or even excites you about these topics.

LITERACY
GATEWAY INSTITUTE

Literacy Gateway Institute, Inc., is an educational solution business focused on success, innovation and access for all learners. The Institute develops and implements learning systems and curricula, improves student performance in content area and standardized tests, and facilitates results-driven interaction between educational institutions and the communities they serve.

literacygatewayinstitute.com